FEARSOME REPTILES

Camilla de la Bédoyère

Created for QED Publishing by Tall Tree Ltd
www.talltreebooks.co.uk
Editors: Jon Richards and Rob Colson
Designer: Jonathan Vipond
Illustration pp18–19:
Mick Posen/www.the-art-agency.co.uk

Copyright © QED Publishing 2012

First published in the UK in 2012 by
QED Publishing
A Quarto Group company
230 City Road
London EC1V 2TT

www.qed-publishing.co.uk

A catalogue record for this book is available from the
British Library.

ISBN 978 1 84835 906 2

Printed in China

Words in **bold** are explained
in the Glossary on page 32.

HOW SCARY?

Look out for this
rating. It will tell
you how scary each
reptile is.

1 – a bit scary

2 – pretty scary

3 – scary

4 – QUICK! RUN AWAY!

5 – AAAARGH! TOO LATE!

CONTENTS

Actual size!

Check out this Puff Adder on page 30

TAIPAN

Snakes are smooth-scaled, slithering **predators**. These reptiles have speed and super senses, and some can inject a deadly **venom** using their fearsome **fangs**.

KILLER FACT

A taipan has enough venom to kill 250,000 mice, 150,000 rats – or 100 people!

The taipan is also called the 'fierce snake'.

The deadly taipan lives in Australian deserts and is the most venomous snake in the world. Taipans belong to a group of snakes that are called elapids.

Like most snakes, taipans hunt small animals to eat, even entering their burrows. They only attack people if they are feeling scared.

A quick death

Most elapids are fast-moving snakes that can strike with lightning speed. When elapid snakes bite their **prey**, venom runs down grooves on a fang's surface or through a canal in the centre of each fang. The venom usually affects the victim's **nervous system**, so it cannot move or breathe.

Taipans have needle-like fangs at the front of their mouths.

REPTILE BITES

Length: Up to 360 cm

Habitat: Forests, deserts and grassland

Where: Northern Australia

Weapons: Needle-sharp fangs with deadly venom

HOW SCARY?

5

KING COBRA

A king cobra puffs out its hood when threatened to make itself look bigger.

The king cobra is the longest of all venomous snakes, and can reach a length of more than five metres. It's so big, a king cobra can raise enough of its body off the ground to look a human in the eye!

As hunters, king cobras have powerful venom and size on their side, but they prey on other snakes, not people. When they are scared, these snakes rear up, spread out their hoods and hiss. Putting on this scary show is a type of defence and it should make most enemies think twice before coming any closer.

REPTILE BITES

Length: 5 m or more

Habitat: Forests, grassland and scrubland

Where: Southeast Asia

Weapons: Fangs with deadly venom

KILLER FACT
King cobras rarely kill people, but Indian cobras attack at least 10,000 people every year in India alone.

Mamba!

Everyone in Africa knows to look out for this snake, which is one of the world's most dangerous predators. Mambas can slither faster than a person can run, are active during daytime and have a deadly bite. Thankfully, mambas normally hunt birds and small animals – not people.

One bite from a mamba can kill an adult human in minutes.

Actual size!

7

KOMODO DRAGON

KILLER FACT
Komodo Island has become a huge wildlife park where the dragons are protected.

REPTILE BITES

Length: Up to 3 m

Habitat: Scrubland and grassland

Where: Komodo Island, Indonesia

Weapons: Big claws and a venomous bite

HOW SCARY?

Few predators are more awesome than the Komodo dragon. These huge reptiles rule the island of Komodo in Indonesia, but there are fewer than 5000 of them left in the wild.

Komodos were not discovered until about 100 years ago.

Komodos are the world's heaviest lizards, and a male can weigh more than an adult human. They have strength rather than speed, and lie in wait for passing prey to **ambush** it. Komodos aren't fussy and will eat almost anything they find, including deer, pigs – and even humans!

Deadly bite

When a Komodo spots its prey, it springs to action and uses its sharp claws to hold the animal down. A quick bite with its sharp teeth allows the Komodo to pass venom into the prey's body. The injured animal runs away, but will soon weaken from its wound. The Komodo can then stroll over and finish its meal.

One side of the Komodo's teeth has jagged **serrations**.

SEA SNAKE

Sea snakes are venomous snakes that have taken to living and hunting underwater. Some sea snakes give birth to live baby snakes in water, while others come onto land to lay their eggs. They all have to come to the surface to breathe.

KILLER FACT
Sea snakes are known for their mild tempers and it is very difficult to make one angry enough to bite.

REPTILE BITES

Length: Up to 110 cm

Habitat: Shallow ocean water

Where: Pacific and Indian Oceans, Arabian Gulf

Weapons: Fangs with a muscle-eating venom

HOW SCARY?

Sea snakes have more powerful venom than any other snakes, but they rarely bite people and have small fangs. Sea snakes feed on small fish and molluscs.

If they do bite, sea snakes inject only a tiny amount of venom and their victims may not even know they have been bitten at first. The venom causes muscles to break down, and death can occur in a few hours.

Sea snakes swim slowly along the ocean floor looking for prey.

Land and sea

Sea snakes called kraits come ashore to **shed** their old skins, to mate and to lay their eggs. The females lay three to 10 eggs in old burrows left by sea birds or under rocks.

Like all snakes, kraits live alone, only coming together to mate.

SALTWATER CROCODILE

When the world's largest reptile decides it is hungry, no one is safe. The saltwater crocodile, or 'saltie', is a fearsome hunter that uses **stealth**, speed and strength to kill.

REPTILE BITES

Length: 250–700 cm

Habitat: Coasts, mangrove swamps, rivers and lakes

Where: Southeast Asia to Australia

Weapons: 64–68 teeth

HOW SCARY?

Saltwater crocodiles live in warm waters in Asia and the Pacific Ocean. These massive crocodilians can grow to at least 5 metres long, but it is thought that some males may grow to more than 7 metres from snout to tail-tip. Despite their huge and heavy bodies, crocodiles can move with great speed on land, and can outrun a human.

Salties hunt fish, mammals and birds. They clamp their jaws around their prey and, gripping tightly, sink below the water. Then the crocodiles begin the 'death roll', and spin their bodies until the prey is drowned.

Salties have 64–68 pointed teeth in their long jaws.

Actual size!

8.5 cm

Death roll

Crocodiles can bite, but they can't chew. Their piercing teeth are perfect for grabbing hold of prey, but they might not kill it. That's why crocodiles perform a death roll.

KILLER FACT
Crocodiles sometimes hunt in groups, which suggests they are smarter than most reptiles.

CORAL SNAKE

Look at the two snakes shown on these pages. Can you tell the difference? The coral snake in the main picture has red and yellow bands that warn predators of its venomous bite, but the milk snake opposite is a harmless copycat.

Coral snakes hunt lizards, snakes, frogs, nesting birds and small mammals.

REPTILE BITES

Length: Up to 90 cm

Habitat: Forests

Where: The Americas

Weapons: Fangs with deadly venom

HOW
SCARY?

The yellow bands on this snake's body are next to the red colour. This means it is a deadly coral snake.

ALLIGATOR

American alligators were so heavily hunted by humans, for their skins, that they were in danger of dying out completely. Today, these impressive predators are protected.

This alligator is hiding under the algae, waiting for unsuspecting prey to pass by.

KILLER FACT

Although they breathe air, alligators can stay underwater for up to six hours at a time.

Like other reptiles, alligators need to keep warm to move at speed, so they spend most of the day floating in water and **basking** in the sun. When they float, alligators can stay almost completely motionless. Just their eyes and the tips of their noses poke above the water – looking for prey and smelling the air.

There are about 40 different types of coral snake, with different patterns of coloured bands. Most live in burrows and only come out at night, so humans rarely encounter these venomous creatures.

Coral snakes need to keep jabbing at a victim to inject all their venom, so although the venom is deadly in large amounts, it is rare for people to die following an attack.

Smart mimic

Milk snakes can bite, but they don't have venom. Their cunning disguise, however, makes them look like venomous coral snakes so predators stay away. A rhyme helps identify some of these colourful snakes: *If red touches yellow, it can kill a fellow, if red touches black, it's a friend of Jack.*

TURN
THE PAGE
TO GET
UP–CLOSE
TO A
DEADLY
ALLIGATOR!

Smaller young alligators often gather together in large groups.

Actual size!

Baby alligators are just 22 cm long when they hatch.

Taking care

Female alligators build huge nests and lay about 45 eggs at a time. After the baby alligators hatch, their mother carefully lifts them in her mouth and takes each one down to the water.

GILA MONSTER

These lizards are called monsters for a good reason – they have venomous bites. Gila monsters mostly use their venom to defend themselves from other animals.

Gilas are slow-moving desert lizards that prey on birds' eggs and bugs. Like other reptiles, these lizards can use their tongues to sense if food is around. When they flick their tongues, they are 'tasting' the air.

20

Big digger

The Mexican beaded lizard also has a venomous bite. It uses its large claws to dig burrows, where it hides. It uses its venom to subdue prey, such as birds and small mammals. Its bite is believed to be harmless to humans.

KiLLER FACT

Some people keep Gila monsters as pets, which is a bad idea. Eight people have died from Gila bites.

Many venomous animals prefer to warn their enemies away, rather than having to fight them. Gila monsters have black bodies with bold patterns of pink, yellow or orange. These colours warn predators that the lizards are venomous.

REPTILE BITES

HOW SCARY?

Length: Up to 50 cm

Habitat: Deserts

Where: Southwestern USA and Mexico

Weapons: Sharp teeth and a venomous bite

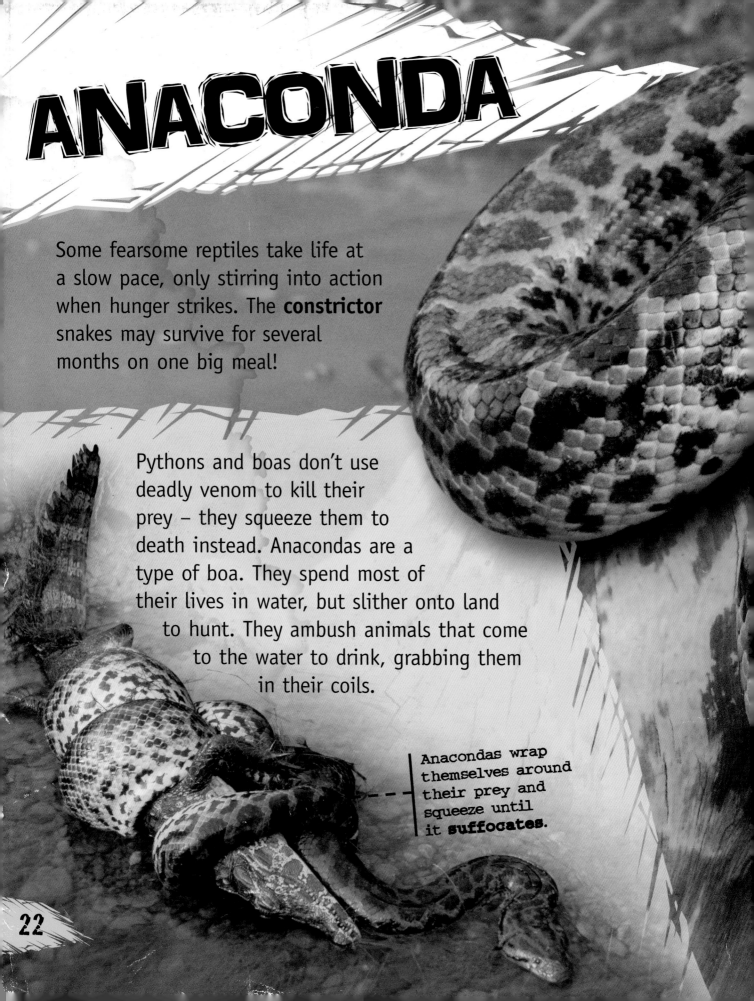

ANACONDA

Some fearsome reptiles take life at a slow pace, only stirring into action when hunger strikes. The **constrictor** snakes may survive for several months on one big meal!

Pythons and boas don't use deadly venom to kill their prey – they squeeze them to death instead. Anacondas are a type of boa. They spend most of their lives in water, but slither onto land to hunt. They ambush animals that come to the water to drink, grabbing them in their coils.

Anacondas wrap themselves around their prey and squeeze until it **suffocates**.

KiLLER FacT

Anacondas don't lay eggs. They give birth to up to 80 young snakes at a time.

A large anaconda is heavier than an adult human.

Massive monsters

Anacondas are big enough to prey on large animals, including caimans, deer and even people. A record-breaking anaconda measured 8.43 metres from head to tail – as long as the net on a tennis court – and 110 centimetres around its middle.

REPTILE BITES

Length: Up to 8.5 m

Habitat: Rainforests, grasslands and rivers

Where: South America

Weapons: Constricting coils

HOW SCARY?

BLACK CAIMAN

When caiman are underwater, special flaps close over their nostrils and ears to stop water from getting in.

Caimans are members of the crocodile and alligator family. Although they are great predators themselves, some types of caiman are close to extinction because humans hunt them for their skins.

KILLER FACT

Caimans attack people for three main reasons: to eat, to defend their homes or to defend their young.

Caimans use their excellent eyesight and sense of smell to hunt fish, waterbirds and turtles. They spend most of the day floating in water, but when they come ashore at night they may hunt mammals, especially **capybaras**, dogs, pigs and deer. They have been known to attack people.

REPTILE BITES

Length: Up to 6 m

Habitat: Rivers and lakes

Where: South America

Weapons: Sharp teeth

The black caiman is the largest predator in the Amazon rainforest

A baby caiman's head is 6–8 cm long

Actual size!

Caring mother

Female black caimans lay up to 60 eggs in a nest near slow-flowing water. They stay on their nest to protect their eggs from predators, and take care of the babies after they **hatch**.

RATTLESNAKE

If you hear the distinctive noise of a rattlesnake shaking its tail, you know it's time to escape – fast! These are supreme hunting serpents with speed, strength and some unbelievable super-skills.

Actual size!

The snake's rattle is at the end of its tail.

Rattlesnakes spend most of the day sunbathing, or hiding under rocks and in burrows. They hunt at dusk, when small mammals come out to find food, and can strike with amazing speed.

HOW SCARY?

When a snake flicks its tongue it is smelling and tasting the air. When the snake pulls its tongue back into its mouth it senses the smell using a special organ in the roof of its mouth.

KILLER FACT

The Western diamondback is the most dangerous of all rattlesnakes, and its bites can prove deadly to humans.

Seeing in the dark

Rattlesnakes can hunt in total darkness. They use special heat-detecting pits to find small animals. This super sense helps the snake to build up a picture of where an animal is, its size, shape and even its movements.

Heat-detecting pit

27

ALLIGATOR SNAPPING TURTLE

This reptilian predator lurks beneath the murky water in swamps. When it lifts its ugly, scaly head above the water, the bad-tempered animal snaps its jaws and does a great impression of a prehistoric monster.

Alligator snapping turtles have one of the nastiest bites of any animal. They grow large and heavy, and live in freshwater where they feed on fish. Snapping turtles can reach the age of 100 or more.

With their spiked shells, these reptiles are known as the dinosaurs of the turtle world.

REPTILE BITES

Length: Up to 80 cm

Habitat: Lakes, rivers and swamps

Where: Southeast USA

Weapons: Scissor-sharp jaws and a vicious bite

HOW SCARY?

Not what it seems!

When a fish approaches a little red, wriggling worm it has no idea it is swimming into the jaws of death. For that is no worm, but a lure – a worm-like lump of flesh inside the turtle's mouth that tempts fish and frogs to come close – SNAP!

KILLER FACT

When the turtle sees food, it fills its lure with blood so that it looks red, plump and very tasty!

29

PUFF ADDER

The body is thick, with a **girth** of up to 40 cm.

When a puff adder is feeling scared it puffs out its body to make itself look larger and hisses. But this snake has little to fear from anyone – it is one of Africa's deadliest snakes.

KiLLER FACT
Puff adders are responsible for nearly two-thirds of all snakebites in Africa.

Puff adders are the most common snakes in Africa, and often live close to humans. They kill more people in Africa than any other kind of snake.

The pattern on its skin keeps the snake well hidden.

Hiding

With brown and cream **camouflage**, puff adders can hide in the undergrowth, waiting to ambush small animals. Their large, heavy bodies slither silently between plants, but when prey is close these cumbersome snakes turn into speedy hunters. If they encounter a human, puff adders can easily deliver enough venom to kill.

A puff adder's long fangs can pierce leather!

GLOSSARY

ambush
A surprise attack made by an animal that has been lying hidden from view.

anti-venom
A medicine that destroys deadly venom in a person's body.

basking
Lying in a warm place, such as sunlight, in order to get warm.

camouflage
A pattern of colours on an animal's body that hides it from predators or prey.

capybara
A large rodent that lives in the grasslands of South America.

constrictor
A kind of snake that kills its prey by squeezing it to death.

fangs
Long, pointed teeth that animals use for biting and tearing flesh.

girth
The distance around a body. The thicker its body, the bigger its girth.

hatch
The breaking out of a baby animal from its egg.

nervous system
A network of nerve cells in an animal's body that carries signals to and from the brain.

predators
Animals that hunt other animals to eat.

prey
Animals that are hunted by predators.

serrations
A series of sharp points that make a saw-like cutting edge.

shed
To take off the outer layer of skin. Snakes shed their skin as they grow.

stealth
Moving carefully and quietly in order to sneak up on prey.

suffocate
To die due to lack of oxygen, caused by not being able to breathe.

venom
A harmful substance that an animal injects into its victim's body by biting or stinging.

TAKING IT FURTHER

What makes a reptile 'scary'? Now it's time for you to decide.

- Choose five scary features, such as speed, size or weapons (such as teeth, claws or jaws) and special powers (such as venom or camouflage).

- Use this book and the Internet to award up to five points for each of a reptile's scary features. Repeat for as many reptiles as you want.

- Turn your results into a table, graph or chart. Add up the totals to get a 'Fearsome Factor' for each reptile.

USEFUL WEBSITES

crocodilian.com
Plenty of information on crocodiles, alligators and caimans.

www.reptilegardens.com
An introduction to reptiles of all types and sizes.

www.sciencedaily.com
For the latest exciting news on science from around the world.

www.arkive.org
Essential information on endangered animals, including reptiles.

TOP 5 DEADLY REPTILE FACTS!

- Spitting cobras blind their victims by spraying venom.

- Some prehistoric snakes were as long as a bus and as heavy as a car.

- Horned lizards defend themselves by squirting blood from their eyes.

- Some crocodiles can gallop, chasing their prey at up to 17 km/h.

- About 2.5 million people are bitten by snakes every year.

INDEX